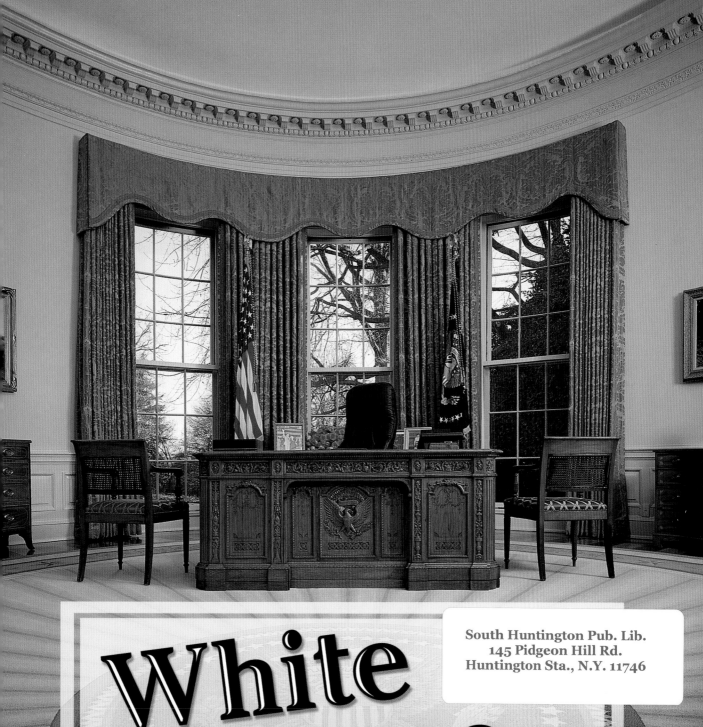

White House

✳ Smithsonian | ◌ Collins

An Imprint of HarperCollinsPublishers

Q&A

J975.3
Rinaldo

Smithsonian Mission Statement

For more than 160 years, the Smithsonian has remained true to its mission, "the increase and diffusion of knowledge." Today the Smithsonian is not only the world's largest provider of museum experiences supported by authoritative scholarship in science, history, and the arts but also an international leader in scientific research and exploration. The Smithsonian offers the world a picture of America, and America a picture of the world.

Special thanks to Lisa Kathleen Graddy, Deputy Chair, Division of Politics and Reform, National Museum of American History, Smithsonian Institution, for her invaluable contribution to this book.

This book was created by **jacob packaged goods LLC** (www.jpgglobal.com)
Written by: Denise Rinaldo
Creative: Ellen Jacob, Sarah L. Thomson, Dawn Camner, Andrea Curley

Photo credits: title page: White House Historical Association (White House Collection); **page 3:** Robert Knudsen/John F. Kennedy Presidential Library; **pages 4–5:** Eric Long © Smithsonian Institution; **page 5, inset:** Jimmy Carter Library; **page 6:** William Winstanley, courtesy Smithsonian American Art Museum, Smithsonian Institution; **page 7:** Library of Congress, 2001698951; **pages 8–9:** White House Historical Association (White House Collection); **page 9, left:** Library of Congress, 96525381; **right:** Library of Congress, 2002719747; **page 10:** White House Historical Association (White House Collection); **page 11:** White House Historical Association (White House Collection); **page 12, inset:** National Portrait Gallery, Smithsonian Institution; transfer from the National Gallery of Art; gift of Mrs. Augustus Vincent Tack, 1952; **pages 12–13:** Harry S. Truman Library; **pages 14–15:** © Charles Ommanney/Contact Press Images; **page 15, inset:** © Charles Ommanney/Contact Press Images; **page 18, inset:** *Harper's Weekly*; **pages 18–19:** Photo by Bruce White, © White House Historical Association; **page 20:** White House Historical Association (White House Collection); **page 21:** William J. Clinton Presidential Library; **page 22:** Courtesy of Gerald R. Ford Presidential Library; **page 23:** White House Historical Association (White House Collection), **page 24, inset:** White House Historical Association; **pages 24–25:** Robert Knudsen/John F. Kennedy Presidential Library; **page 26:** White House Historical Association (White House Collection); **page 27:** NARA; **pages 28–29:** White House Historical Association (White House Collection); **page 29, inset:** John F. Kennedy Library; **page 30:** Library of Congress, 95504424; **page 31:** Library of Congress, 96512169; **page 32, inset:** White House Historical Association (White House Collection); **pages 32–33:** White House Historical Association (White House Collection); **page 34:** Library of Congress, 2002713183; **page 35, left:** Ollie Atkins Collection, Special Collections & Archives, George Mason University Libraries; **center:** Robert Knudsen/John F. Kennedy Presidential Library; **right:** William J. Clinton Presidential Library; **page 36, left:** William Phillips for the White House Historical Association; **right:** William J. Clinton Presidential Library; **page 37:** © APImages; **page 38:** Robert Knudsen/John F. Kennedy Presidential Library; **page 43:** Courtesy Ronald Reagan Library; **page 46:** Robert Knudsen/John F. Kennedy Presidential Library

Contents

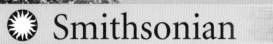

What is the White House?

It's a **mansion** at 1600 Pennsylvania Avenue in Washington, DC—but it is also much more!

The White House has been the home and office of the president of the United States for more than 200 years.

The White House is where presidents make decisions that change the course of history. Where was President Abraham Lincoln when he commanded the **Union** army in the war that ended

President Jimmy Carter watches his daughter, Amy, and one of her younger relatives play in her tree house on the White House lawn.

The White House gets a fresh coat of paint every four years.

slavery in the United States? In the White House, of course.

The White House is also where presidents' families live and where their children grow up. Amy Carter, the daughter of President Jimmy Carter, had a tree house in the White House backyard (which is called the South Lawn).

When the White House was built, no one imagined a tree house in the garden. In fact, when the building was finished, it wasn't even called the White House—because it wasn't white!

Who designed the White House?

It was 1789, and the United States capital would soon be moving from Philadelphia to Washington, DC. President George Washington decided that the country needed a house for the president. A contest was held to find the best design. Washington chose the winner—James Hoban, a young Irish immigrant—in 1792. When George Washington died in 1799, the White House still wasn't finished. The man who came up with the idea for the White House never even spent the night there.

Washington personally supervised the planning and construction of the White House before his death.

Was the president's house always called the White House?

The White House started out grayish brown, the color of the sandstone used to build it. Early on, the building was given a coat of **white-wash**. Soon people were calling it the White House. In 1901, President Theodore Roosevelt made the nickname official. He had "White House" printed on his presidential stationery.

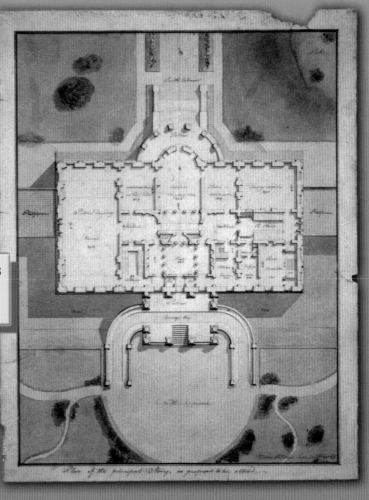

This drawing from 1803 shows the plan for the main floor of the White House.

Who was the first president to live in the White House?

John Adams moved in on November 1, 1800. After spending his second night in the White House, Adams wrote a letter to his wife, Abigail. "May none but honest and wise men ever rule under this roof," he said. Those words are now carved above the fireplace in the State Dining Room.

First Lady Abigail Adams soon joined her husband in the White House. (The **first lady** is the president's wife, just as the **first family** is the president's family.) She didn't enjoy living there—probably because the

The East Room is now one of the fanciest rooms in the White House, but when Abigail Adams lived there the walls weren't plastered and her servants hung laundry there to dry.

house was still under construction. Many of the windows had no glass, and people had to walk up wooden planks to get to the front door.

In 1809, when Thomas Jefferson was president, the house was finally finished. Then, five years later, it went up in flames.

When First Lady Abigail Adams and President John Adams moved into the White House, only six of the thirty-six rooms were finished.

Why did the White House burn down?

Because the British set it on fire. It was the night of August 24, 1814, and the United States was at war with England. **Redcoats**—British soldiers—stormed the White House and set it ablaze. Flames lit the night sky so brightly that people saw the glow from fifty miles away.

First Lady Dolley Madison escaped out the back just minutes before the British arrived. She had stayed behind—even after White House guards had fled—to save a precious painting of George Washington. The portrait is still on display in the White House.

This painting shows Dorothea "Dolley" Payne Todd Madison in 1804, five years before her husband was elected president.

After the fire, all that remained of the White House was the walls. The White House was rebuilt to be almost the same as before. But as the years went by, the building slowly changed.

The reconstructed White House was finished in the autumn of 1817.

British redcoats watch as the White House burns.

SMITHSONIAN LINK
See a portrait of George Washington similar to the one that Dolley Madison rescued: www.npg.si.edu/exh/gw/lands.htm

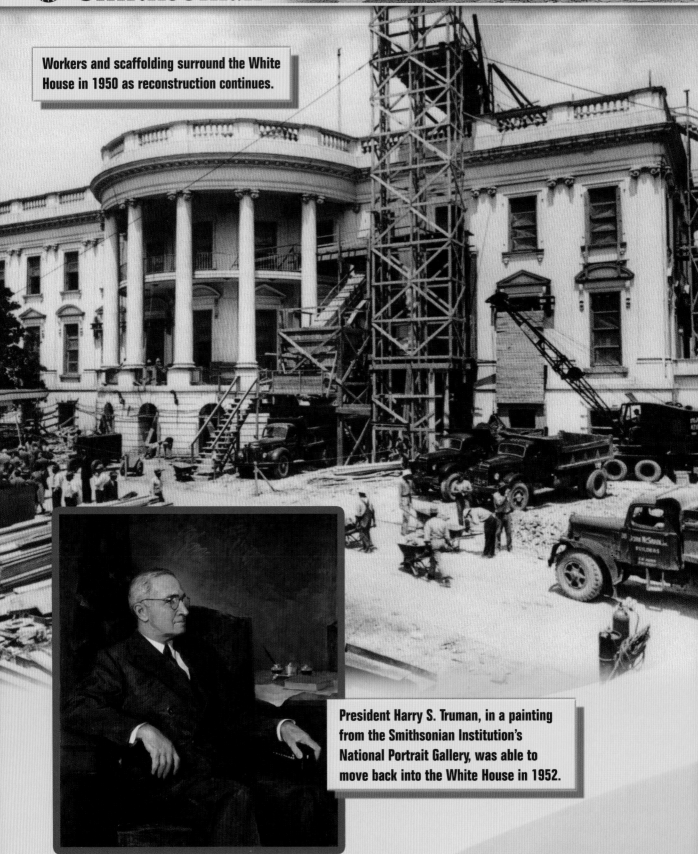

Workers and scaffolding surround the White House in 1950 as reconstruction continues.

President Harry S. Truman, in a painting from the Smithsonian Institution's National Portrait Gallery, was able to move back into the White House in 1952.

How has the White House changed?

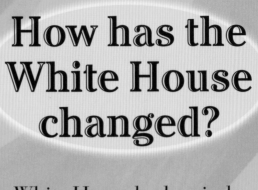

At first, the White House had no indoor plumbing, no electric lights (they hadn't been invented yet!), and no furnace.

In 1833, President Andrew Jackson had running water installed. President James K. Polk put in gas lamps in 1848. Before that, there were only candles and oil lamps. The first electric lights were switched on in 1891.

By the 1900's, the White House was starting to wear out.

Some things were done to fix it, but one day, while Harry S. Truman was president, a piano leg broke through the ceiling. It turned out that the whole house was unsafe. The Trumans moved across the street while the inside of the White House was rebuilt.

When you walk into the White House today, the rooms are laid out pretty much the way they were when the rebuilding was finished in 1952.

How do you get into the White House?

There are four ways in. The north door is on Pennsylvania Avenue. It is famous as the place where a president leaving his job hands off power to the new president. If you find yourself standing at the north door with a president shaking your hand and saying, "Welcome to your new home," that's good news for you!

The south door is right next to a helicopter landing pad. It's used by the first family when they leave on a trip or by important visitors who zoom in by chopper. The east door is where you'd enter if you took a tour of the White House.

What about the west door? That's the door the president walks through to get to the most important room in the White House—in a **wing** that isn't even in the main part of the building.

President and Laura Bush often greet important visitors at the White House's formal entrance, the north door.

A worker prepares for visitors by vacuuming the red carpet leading to the south door of the White House.

What is the most important room in the White House?

When it comes to political power, the Oval Office is the place to be. It's the president's office, the room where he goes to work on most days.

The Oval Office is in the West Wing, built when Theodore Roosevelt was president. Before then, the president's office was on the second floor, where the first family lives. But Roosevelt had six kids—noisy ones! There wasn't room on the floor for the president, his **staff**, and his family, so Roosevelt had the West Wing built. (It was rebuilt later, when Theodore Roosevelt's fifth cousin, Franklin Delano Roosevelt, was president.)

The Oval Office is really oval shaped.

The Resolute desk, seen here in the Oval Office, was given by Britain's Queen Victoria to President Rutherford B. Hayes in 1880.

The East Room has hosted events ranging from formal balls to presidential farewells and senior proms.

President Abraham Lincoln's coffin is surrounded by mourners in this 1865 drawing of the East Room.

What is the most historic room in the White House?

The East Room—no contest! Remember that painting of George Washington that Dolley Madison rescued? It's hanging in the East Room, the only object that remains from the original White House.

During the Civil War, when the Union fought the **Confederacy**, Union troops camped out in the East Room. After Abraham Lincoln was assassinated, his body **lay in state** there so people could pay their respects.

Richard M. Nixon, the only president who ever gave up his job before his term was over, said good-bye to his staff in the East Room. Susan Ford, daughter of President Gerald Ford, had her senior prom there.

Who takes care of the White House?

Lots of people, about a hundred of them. There's an electrician, a plumber, six butlers, and a cook (called a pastry chef) who makes only desserts. The chief usher oversees everybody. It's his or her job to know every nook and cranny of the White House. Presidents come and go, but ushers often keep their jobs through several presidencies.

Another important part of taking care of the White House is keeping it safe. The Secret Service, a special police force, protects the White House and the first family. It uses everything from dogs to high-tech

Pastry chef Roland Mesnier, who baked for presidents for twenty-five years, slides a batch of cookies into a White House oven.

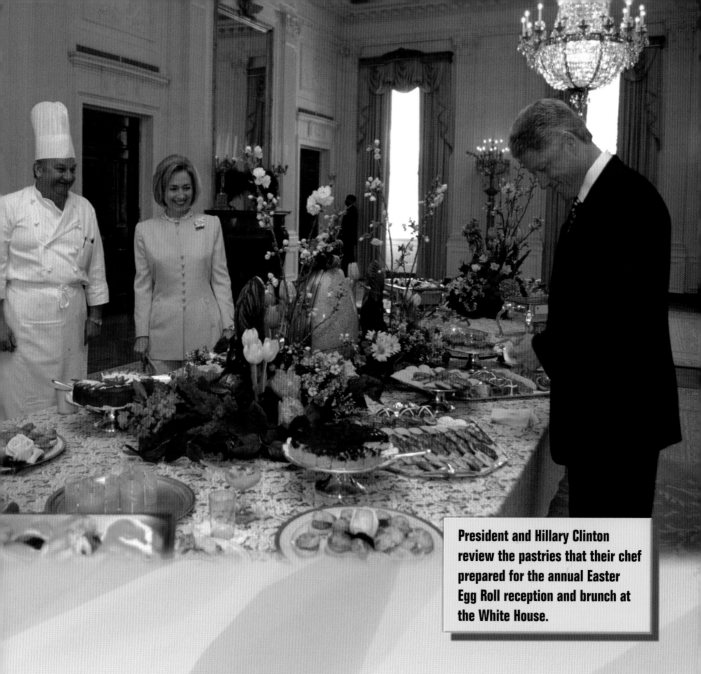

President and Hillary Clinton review the pastries that their chef prepared for the annual Easter Egg Roll reception and brunch at the White House.

equipment. If you visit, you may see Secret Service agents on the roof. Don't worry. They're always up there, keeping an eye on things.

White House security is extra high when there are special events—such as visits from foreign leaders and state dinners.

What is a state dinner?

It's a dinner party that the president throws for a head of another country. Usually, state dinners are held in the State Dining Room.

If you ever get an invitation to a state dinner, definitely go! Most presidents hold only a few. Politicians in Washington, DC, dream about making the guest list.

The food at state dinners is always ultrafancy—and just wait for dessert! The pastry chef creates a sweet treat that honors the home country of the dinner guests. In honor of Kenya (in 2003, when George W. Bush was president), it was sugar giraffes. To honor the United Kingdom (in 1998, when Bill Clinton was president), there were tiny chocolate copies of Big Ben, a famous clock in London.

State dinners don't end when the eating does. After dessert, guests often dance in the East Room or take a stroll in the Rose Garden.

President Ford danced with England's Queen Elizabeth II after a state dinner in her honor in July 1976.

The White House State Dining Room has space for 140 guests. Here, it is set up for a state dinner.

The handprints of children and grandchildren of presidents are mounted in some of the paving stones of the White House Children's Garden.

What is the Rose Garden?

It's where you'll be if the president decides to honor you with an outdoor ceremony at the White House.

The Rose Garden got its name in 1913 when First Lady Ellen Wilson planted the first roses there. About fifty years later, President John F. Kennedy put in a lawn with room for a thousand folding chairs. Since then, crowds have gathered in the Rose Garden to see presidents honor everyone from World Series winners to astronauts to National Teachers of the Year.

The Rose Garden is just outside the Oval Office. This is the way it looked when John F. Kennedy was president.

The Rose Garden isn't the only White House garden. The building is surrounded by greenery—eighteen acres of it! There's even a Children's Garden with a goldfish pond and an apple tree for climbing.

Many other White House gardens were put in under the direction of first ladies.

How have first ladies changed the White House?

Almost every first lady has left her mark on the White House.

Abigail Fillmore was a teacher before she moved into the White House. She loved reading and couldn't believe how few books were in her new home. She solved the problem by setting up a White House library. First families have been using it ever since.

Presidents always had their portraits painted. Edith Roosevelt, the wife of President Theodore Roosevelt, thought first ladies ought to be there, too. So she started a first ladies' picture gallery. Caroline Harrison, who was married to President William Henry Harrison, began to collect china for the White House.

First Lady Edith Roosevelt started a portrait gallery of presidents' wives.

Jacqueline Kennedy changed the inside of the White House, filling it with historical art and fine furniture. Then she went on TV and gave a tour. For the first time, millions of Americans caught a glimpse of how the first family lived. Pat Nixon started White House tours for people who are blind or deaf, or who use wheelchairs.

SMITHSONIAN LINK
Visit this to see dresses that first ladies have worn to important events:
www.smithsonianlegacies.si.edu/exhibit.cfm

First Lady Jacqueline Kennedy shows the State Dining Room during a television tour she led in 1962.

Where does the first family live?

On the top two floors of the White House. The living area has more than two dozen rooms, so there's always plenty of room for guests!

Some of the rooms are almost like museums. One, called the Lincoln Bedroom, was used as an office by Abraham Lincoln. Some of the furniture there is his, but he never slept in the bed.

Lucky visitors get to spend the night there (and some go home saying they sensed Lincoln's ghost).

Other rooms are more ordinary: the first family's kitchen, where "first kids" can whip up midnight snacks, and a living room, where they can play video games. When a new president is elected, the whole family looks through pictures of furniture from the White House storage rooms. Everybody—adults and kids alike—can pick out exactly what he or she wants.

The Lincoln Bedroom, furnished with items once used by President Abraham Lincoln, is a favorite place for White House guests to sleep.

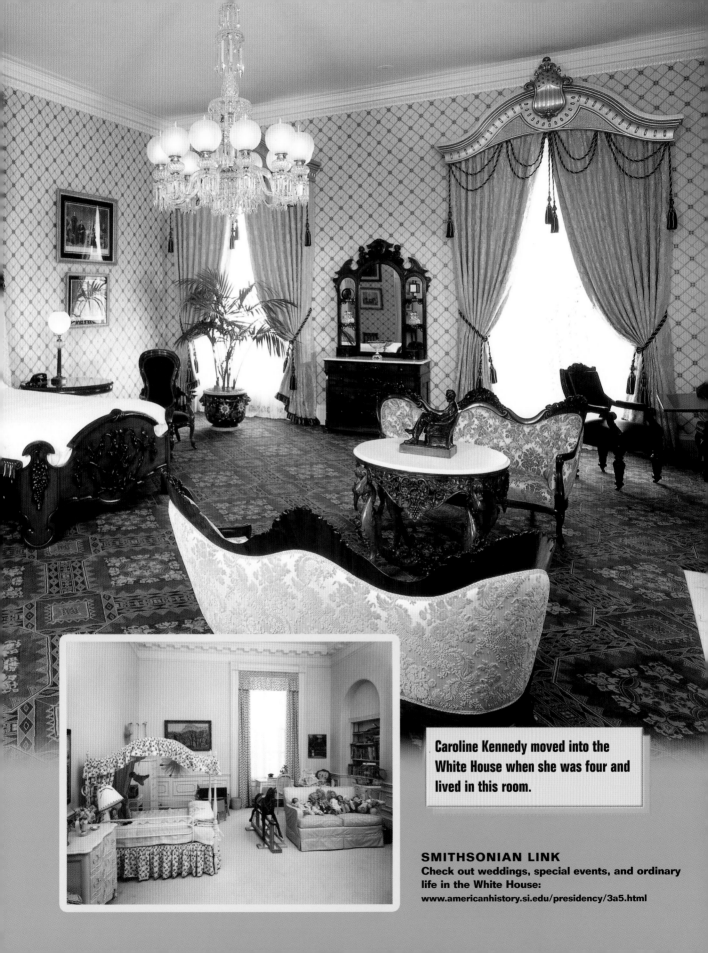

Caroline Kennedy moved into the
White House when she was four and
lived in this room.

SMITHSONIAN LINK
Check out weddings, special events, and ordinary
life in the White House:
www.americanhistory.si.edu/presidency/3a5.html

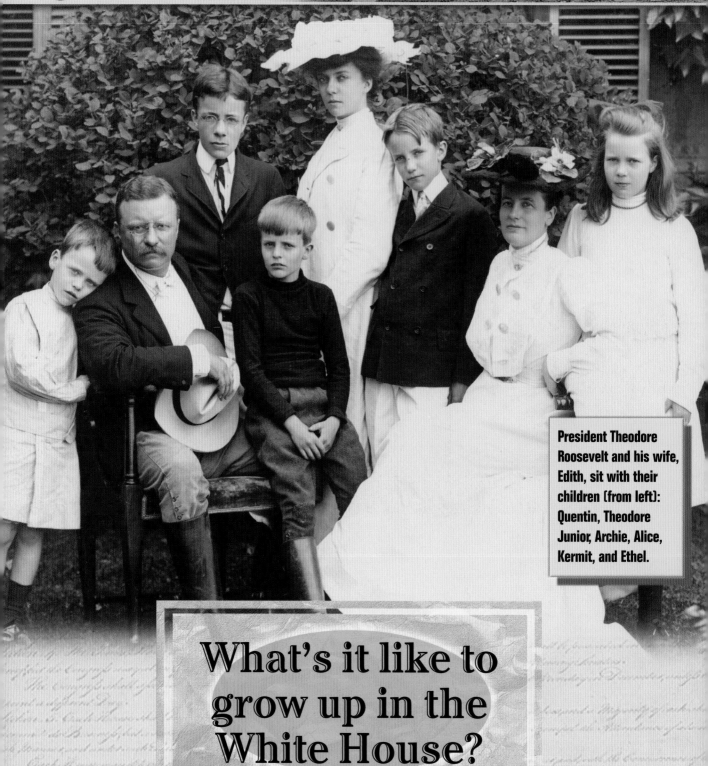

President Theodore Roosevelt and his wife, Edith, sit with their children (from left): Quentin, Theodore Junior, Archie, Alice, Kermit, and Ethel.

What's it like to grow up in the White House?

It can be tough for a kid to live in the White House. Everybody in the whole country knows all about you. That doesn't keep first kids from acting like kids, though.

The wildest White House kids had to be President Theodore Roosevelt's six. They roller-skated in the East Room, teetered down the halls on stilts, and played leapfrog on the furniture, and they may have hurled spitballs at a portrait of President Andrew Jackson.

That's not the worst thing a first kid has done. Chester A. Arthur's son was reportedly caught skinny-dipping in a White House fountain. And when the Civil War ended, Abraham Lincoln's son Tad got extremely excited—so excited that he waved a flag from out of a White House window. Unfortunately, it was the flag of the Confederacy—when his father was the head of the *Union* army!

President Lincoln spends a quiet moment with his son Tad.

SMITHSONIAN LINK
See some pictures of White House kids:
www.americanhistory.si.edu/presidency/3a5_c.html

They go for a dip in the pool, play a little tennis, or roll a few balls down the bowling lane. If you live in the White House, you can do all that and more without leaving home.

President Bill Clinton loved the private movie theater. There are four big armchairs, with about forty seats behind them. The kitchen staff is always on hand to make popcorn or whatever other snack the first family is in the mood to munch.

First families also relax in more regular ways. One winter day, President Ronald Reagan brought his grandchildren to the Rose Garden. They built a snowman together.

President Richard M. Nixon had this one-lane bowling alley built in the White House in 1969.

How do first families relax in the White House?

Children sit in the White House movie theater. The four upholstered armchairs with foot rests in front are usually for the president and his guests of honor.

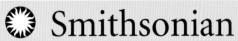

President Warren G. Harding greets his Airedale terrier, Laddie Boy. The lucky hound had White House birthday parties and often sat in on important meetings.

Are pets allowed in the White House?

Of course! Would *you* tell the president, "No pets allowed!"? President Theodore Roosevelt's children practically had a zoo. They owned bears, snakes, guinea pigs, a pony, and a raccoon, plus some dogs and cats! Once, Quentin Roosevelt brought his pony up in the White House elevator. He did it to cheer up his brother, who was sick in bed.

There have been hundreds of other White House pets, from every branch of the animal kingdom.

Top, from left to right: The Nixon family's dogs line up for a photo on the south lawn of their home. President Kennedy's daughter, Caroline, sits on her pony, Macaroni, on the South Lawn. Socks, the Clinton family's famous cat, inspects the colored eggs on the White House lawn during the annual Easter Egg Roll.

How are holidays celebrated at the White House?

There are White House **traditions** for almost every holiday.

On Easter Monday, crowds of kids use spoons to roll eggs across the South Lawn. At Christmas there are beautifully decorated trees.

Just before Thanksgiving, the president **pardons** a turkey. This turkey won't end up on a platter. It will live out its days at a petting farm. The tradition was inspired by President Abraham Lincoln. His son Tad

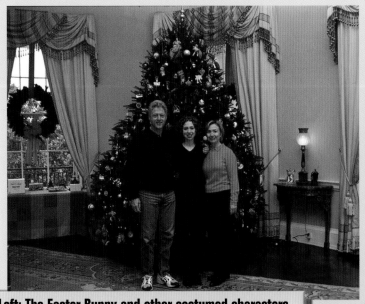

Left: The Easter Bunny and other costumed characters are part of the White House Easter celebration.
Above: The Clinton family—Bill, daughter Chelsea, and Hillary—pose for an informal picture with their Christmas tree in January 1999.

had a turkey that was like a pet, and Lincoln let the bird live instead of serving it for dinner.

For many years, New Year's Day was visiting day at the White House. Anyone could walk right in. The tradition ended in 1932, when President Herbert Hoover decided the crowds were too big to handle.

Today you can still visit the White House, but you can't just drop in.

SMITHSONIAN LINK
To see pictures about the annual Easter Egg Roll and other holiday festivities at the White House, visit this site:
www.americanhistory.si.edu/presidency/3a2.html

President George W. Bush pets Liberty as he pardons the Thanksgiving turkey in the Rose Garden in 2001.

When you visit the White House you will get to see the South Portico.

Can anyone visit the White House?

To tour the White House, you have to make a reservation at least two months ahead. You'll get to see the public rooms, including the East Room and the State Dining Room. Will you see the president? Probably not. But you never know!

What happens when you write to the White House?

You get a letter back. The White House receives thousands of letters from kids every day. Volunteers and staff members open every single one, and usually send a photograph in return.

All mail sent to the White House is kept in the National Archives (the government office that preserves important papers). So when you write to the White House, your letter becomes part of history!

Write to:

**The White House
1600 Pennsylvania Avenue NW
Washington, DC 20500**

DEAR MR. PRESIDENT, I VISITED THE WHITE HOUSE LAST WEEK AND THOUGHT IT WAS VERY BEAUTIFUL. AD FUN SEEING THE

When did each president live in the White House?

Geororge Washington, the first president, never lived in the White House. But every president after Washington has lived there—and has made a contribution to the history that it represents. Here is a list of all the presidents who lived in the White House, along with the years they served and something about what happened when they lived there.

2. **John Adams, 1797–1801:** He was the first president to live in the White House—even though it was still being built when he moved in.

3. **Thomas Jefferson, 1801–1809:** His grandson James Madison Randolph was the first baby born in the White House.

4. **James Madison, 1809–1817:** During the War of 1812, he and his family were driven out of the White House by British troops, who set the house on fire.

5. **James Monroe, 1817–1825:** He and First Lady Elizabeth Monroe bought fancy furniture from France for the White House. (Some of it is still there.)

6. **John Quincy Adams, 1825–1829:** He planted many trees, flowers, and other plants around the White House.

7. **Andrew Jackson, 1829–1837:** For his first inauguration, he held an open house at the White House, and twenty thousand people showed up. The crowd got out of hand and he had to flee to a hotel.

8. **Martin Van Buren, 1837–1841:** He added a hot-air heating system to the White House.

9. **William Henry Harrison, 1841:** He was the first president to die in office (he was president for only thirty days) and the first to lie in state in the White House.

10. John Tyler, 1841–1845: His second wife, Julia, was famous for hosting lavish White House parties.

11. James K. Polk, 1845–1849: His wife, Sarah, didn't allow any dancing or card-playing in the White House.

12. Zachary Taylor, 1849–1850: A hero of the Mexican War, he kept his horse, Old Whitey, in the White House stable.

13. Millard Fillmore, 1850–1853: He added pianos and a harp to the collection of musical instruments in the White House.

14. Franklin Pierce, 1853–1857: He had a permanent bathtub installed in the White House. (Before that, presidents bathed in portable tubs that were filled from kettles of hot water.)

15. James Buchanan, 1857–1861: The only bachelor to serve as president, he brought in his niece Harriet Lane to serve as official hostess.

16. Abraham Lincoln, 1861–1865: He gave his two youngest sons pet goats that were allowed to walk around in the White House.

17. Andrew Johnson, 1865–1869: During his term, the tradition of hanging presidents' portraits in the White House was started.

18. Ulysses S. Grant, 1869–1877: He put a billiard table in the White House and had the East Room redecorated.

19. Rutherford B. Hayes, 1877–1881: He started the tradition of the annual Easter Egg Roll.

20. James Garfield, 1881: He ordered an elevator for the White House but was assassinated before it was put in.

21. Chester A. Arthur, 1881–1885: He hired designer Louis Comfort Tiffany to redecorate the White House. Tiffany's changes included installing elegant ceilings and a large stained-glass screen.

22, 24. Grover Cleveland, 1885–1889 and 1893–1897: He was the only president to be married in the White House. He was also the only one to leave it after one term, get elected again, and come back four years later.

23. Benjamin Harrison, 1889–1893: He put up the first Christmas tree inside the White House.

25. William McKinley, 1897–1901: He was assassinated and lay in state in the East Room.

26. Theodore Roosevelt, 1901–1909: His oldest child, Alice, carried her snake, Emily Spinach, around the White House.

27. William Howard Taft, 1909–1913: This 300-pound-plus president had a special bathtub installed in the White House that was big enough for four regular-sized men.

32. **Franklin Delano Roosevelt, 1933–1945:** This president lived in the White House longer than any other (twelve years) and rebuilt the West Wing.

33. **Harry S. Truman, 1945–1953:** The inside of the White House was rebuilt while he was president, and he lived across the street in Blair House, a guest house for official visitors. He also added the Truman Balcony.

34. **Dwight D. Eisenhower, 1953–1961:** He liked to barbecue and to hit golf balls on the White House lawn.

35. **John F. Kennedy, 1961–1963:** When his kids, Caroline and John Jr., lived in the White House, Caroline had a pony named Macaroni.

28. **Woodrow Wilson, 1913–1921:** Instead of having men cut the grass, he let a flock of sheep graze on the White House lawn.

29. **Warren G. Harding, 1921–1923:** This president liked to play poker; he once lost a set of fancy White House dishes in a card game.

29. **Calvin Coolidge, 1923–1929:** A glass sunroom with a great view of Washington, DC, was added to the top floor of the White House during his term.

31. **Herbert Hoover, 1929–1933:** Soon after she moved in, First Lady Lou Hoover began to study and catalog the White House's furniture and decorations.

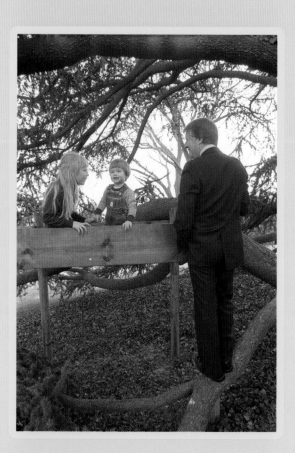

36. Lyndon B. Johnson, 1963–1969: He brought Texas-style barbecues to the White House for the first time, and held a wedding for his older daughter there.

37. Richard M. Nixon, 1969–1974: With First Lady Pat Nixon, he made a special effort to bring American antique furniture and paintings into the White House.

38. Gerald Ford, 1974–1977: He had an outdoor swimming pool built on the White House grounds.

39. Jimmy Carter, 1977–1981: To show the importance of saving energy, he had solar heating panels installed on the roof of the West Wing.

40. Ronald Reagan, 1981–1989: He and First Lady Nancy Reagan redecorated the White House family quarters.

41. George H. W. Bush, 1989–1993: This president's dog, Millie, wrote an autobiography while living in the White House (with the help of First Lady Barbara Bush).

42. Bill Clinton, 1993–2001: In 2000 he hosted celebrations for the 200th anniversary of the White House.

43. George W. Bush, 2001–present: He lives in the White House with his wife, Laura; his cat, Willie; and two Scottish terriers, Barney and Miss Beazley.

After a snowstorm in January 1985, President Reagan builds a snowman in the White House Rose Garden with his son Michael and his grandchildren.

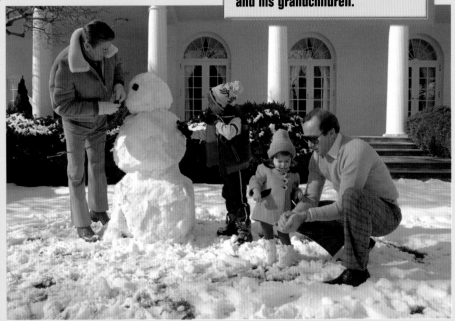

SMITHSONIAN LINK
See George Washington's tent, Thomas Jefferson's musket, and one of the first teddy bears (named for Theodore Roosevelt) at this site:
www.smithsonianlegacies.si.edu/exhibit.cfm

Meet the Curator
William "Bill" G. Allman
WHITE HOUSE CURATOR

Why did you become a curator and historian? Did anything or anyone from your childhood influence your decision?

I have always been interested in history but also in collecting things. As a kid, I collected coins, stamps, and rocks and such but also books. My family loved to travel to national parks, monuments, and historic sites. When I was asked once how I knew the answer to some obscure question, a young friend commented, "Because he's the curator, dude." In her mind, it was natural for a curator to be a collector of answers.

When you were growing up, did you want to be a historian?

I always was interested in history and geography, but I never imagined to what career that would bring me. I thought I would go into teaching history. Museum work was not an obvious path.

If you couldn't be a historian, what would you want to be?

I probably would be a teacher. I still might try

some kind of teaching after my museum career is over.

How did you get to be the curator at the White House?

A summer job with the National Park Service placed me in the facility where White House furnishings were stored. My research about the things there led me to the curator's office at the White House.

Did you read books or watch TV shows about the White House? Which ones?

In elementary school, I read history books and biographies, often ones about the presidents. I was encouraged to read more fiction in order to be a well-rounded student.

How can kids get interested in your field?

Museums cover many topics. So a kid interested in science, art, history, and many other subjects can study for a museum career. For me there's something fascinating about seeing the "real thing"—whether it may be paintings, furniture, rocks, airplanes, or baskets—that make many museums, historic sites, and even zoos so important.

What kind of education and training did you need for your job?

Learning how to write clearly, research thoroughly, and enjoy a broad range of subjects helps prepare one for my kind of job. Some of the specific education you need you may get on the job, but many colleges now offer programs in museum studies to help you apply your knowledge of a particular subject to a museum operation.

What work do you do most days?

We take care of all of the possessions of the White House. We collect, study, document, and write about or help others write about these objects. Some of these things may be used in the rooms open to the public; others in the first family's private quarters. We also answer questions about the White House and its history.

What do you like most about your job?

Unlike most other historic houses, the history of the White House never stops evolving because every new president and first family adds to it. It is nice to know that our office helps record this history.

Where do you get the furniture for the White House? What happens to the furniture when a president leaves office? Can presidents select their own furniture?

In the 1800s, presidents could sell off old White House property (they would have a garage sale of sorts). Today the contents of the White House—paintings, sculpture, furniture, lighting fixtures, fireplace equipment, rugs, china, glass, and silver—is a permanent museum collection for use in both the public and private rooms of the house.

Which is your favorite room in the White House?

I think I like the Blue Room best. It has a very unusual oval shape. Many of things in the room were bought by President James Monroe in 1817 after the British burned the White House during the War of 1812. Some things have been there ever since. The chairs, however, were sold in 1860 (back when there was no curator), but some have come back since 1961 (when the curator's position was created).

Can the presidents go to the kitchen and get a snack anytime they want?

The residence staff is ready and willing to provide almost any service needed by the president, first lady, members of the first family, or their guests. If he likes, the president always can go to the kitchen in the private quarters and make a little something for himself.

Glossary

Confederacy—The 11 southern states that seceded from the United States in 1860 and 1861 and formed the Confederate States of America.

first family—The family of a president.

first lady—The wife of a president, or sometimes a daughter, daughter-in-law, or niece who acts as the White House hostess. (Would the husband of a president be called the first man? The first husband? We don't know yet, because all presidents so far have been men. But someday we'll find out!)

lying in state—The tradition of putting a coffin on view so that the public can pay their respects to a person who has died. The coffins used to be open, but now they are usually closed. Presidents who die in office usually lie in state in the East Room.

mansion—A very large house.

pardon—To free a person or animal from a punishment. Every year, the president pardons a turkey, freeing it from being killed and eaten on Thanksgiving Day.

redcoats—A nickname for British soldiers, whose red coats were part of their uniforms. Redcoats set the White House on fire during the War of 1812.

staff—A group of people who work for the same person or company. The people who work for the president make up his staff.

traditions—Customs that are handed down through the years. The Easter Egg Roll is a White House custom.

Union— The states that remained part of the United States during the Civil War.

whitewash—Old-fashioned white paint usually made from limestone and water.

wing—A part of a building that sticks out from the main section. The White House has two wings: the East Wing and the West Wing.

More to See and Read

Websites

There are links to many wonderful web pages in this book. But the web is constantly growing and changing, so we cannot guarantee that the sites we recommend will be available. If the site you want is no longer there, you can always find your way to plenty of information about the White House through the main Smithsonian website: www.si.edu.

Read more about the White House and the presidency at the official White House website for kids: www.whitehousekids.gov. Click on "Tours" for a video tour of the White House.

Find answers to your questions about the history of the White House at the website of the White House Historical Society: www.whitehousehistory.org

Learn all about how the United States government works at this website for kids, hosted by a cartoon version of Benjamin Franklin: http://bensguide.gpo.gov

Take a virtual historical tour through the White House: www.whitehousehistory.org/02/02.html

Visit this site to learn more about first kids and presidential pets: www.whitehousehistory.org/04/subs/04_a01_d.html

Suggested Reading

The White House: An Illustrated History by Catherine O'Neill Grace, published in cooperation with the White House Historical Association. A history of the White House from its early days to today.

It Happened in the White House: Extraordinary Tales from America's Most Famous Home by Kathleen Karr, illustrated by Paul Meisel. Amazing true stories about life in the White House.

Wackiest White House Pets by Kathryn Gibbs Davis, illustrated by David A. Johnson. All about the dogs, cats, parrots, badgers, and other creatures that have lived in the White House.

A Christmas Tree in the White House by Gary Hines, illustrated by Alexandra Wallner. A picture book about what President Theodore Roosevelt's kids did when their father said they couldn't have a Christmas tree (because he thought it was bad for the environment to cut one down).

Index